Recipe ....

Date ....

Serves .... Preperation time .... Cooking time ....

Ingredients

Directions

_____

_____

_____

_____

_____

_____

_____

_____

_____

_____

_____

_____

Notes:

Air Fryer

TEMPERATURE

MINUTES

Protein:	Cals:	Carbs:	Fat:

Check Box ✓	Vegitarian:	Vegan:	Gluten free:	Contains Nuts:	Lactose
	☐	☐	☐	☐	☐

Recipe ----------------------------------

Date ....

Serves .... Preperation time .... Cooking time ....

Ingredients

Directions

Air Fryer

TEMPERATURE

MINUTES

Notes:

Protein:	Cals:	Carbs:	Fat:

Check Box ✓	Vegitarian:	Vegan:	Gluten free:	Contains Nuts:	Lactose
	☐	☐	☐	☐	☐

Recipe ----------------------------- ❤❤

Date ....

Serves .... Preperation time .... Cooking time ....

Ingredients   ## Directions

_____   _____
_____   _____
_____   _____
_____   _____
_____   _____
_____   _____
_____   _____
_____   _____
_____   _____
_____   _____
_____   _____
_____   _____
_____   Notes:
Air Fryer   _____
_____   _____
TEMPERATURE   _____
MINUTES

Protein:	Cals:	Carbs:	Fat:

Check Box ✓	Vegitarian:	Vegan:	Gluten free:	Contains Nuts:	Lactose
	☐	☐	☐	☐	☐

Recipe ....

Date ....

Serves .... Preperation time .... Cooking time ....

Ingredients

Directions

Air Fryer

TEMPERATURE

MINUTES

Notes:

Protein: Cals: Carbs: Fat:

Check Box ✓	Vegitarian:	Vegan:	Gluten free:	Contains Nuts:	Lactose
	☐	☐	☐	☐	☐

Recipe ------------------------------

Date ....

Serves .... Preperation time .... Cooking time ....

Ingredients

Directions

Air Fryer

TEMPERATURE

MINUTES

Notes:

Protein: _____ **Cals:** _____ **Carbs:** _____ **Fat:** _____

Check Box ✓

Vegitarian:	Vegan:	Gluten free:	Contains Nuts:	Lactose
☐	☐	☐	☐	☐

Recipe ....

Date ....

Serves .... Preperation time .... Cooking time ....

Ingredients

Directions

Notes:

Air Fryer

TEMPERATURE

MINUTES

Protein:	Cals:	Carbs:	Fat:

Check Box ✓

Vegitarian:	Vegan:	Gluten free:	Contains Nuts:	Lactose
☐	☐	☐	☐	☐

Recipe ----------------------------

Date ....

Serves .... **Preperation time** .... **Cooking time** ....

Ingredients   ## Directions

Air Fryer

TEMPERATURE

MINUTES

Notes:

Protein: **Cals:**   **Carbs:**   **Fat:**

Check Box ✓ | Vegitarian: | Vegan: | Gluten free: | Contains Nuts: | Lactose

Recipe ....

Date ....

Serves .... Preperation time .... Cooking time ....

Ingredients

Directions

Air Fryer

TEMPERATURE

MINUTES

Notes:

Protein:	Cals:	Carbs:	Fat:

Check Box ✓	Vegitarian:	Vegan:	Gluten free:	Contains Nuts:	Lactose
	☐	☐	☐	☐	☐

Recipe ------------------------------

Date ....

Serves .... Preperation time .... Cooking time ....

Ingredients

Directions

Notes:

Air Fryer

TEMPERATURE

MINUTES

Protein: **Cals:**   **Carbs:**   **Fat:**

Check Box ✓   Vegitarian: Vegan: Gluten free: Contains Nuts: Lactose

Recipe ....

Date ....

Serves .... Preperation time .... Cooking time ....

Ingredients

Directions

Air Fryer

TEMPERATURE

MINUTES

Notes:

Protein:	Cals:	Carbs:	Fat:	

Check Box ✓

Vegitarian:	Vegan:	Gluten free:	Contains Nuts:	Lactose
☐	☐	☐	☐	☐

Recipe ----------------------------

Date ....

Serves .... Preperation time .... Cooking time ....

Ingredients

Directions

Air Fryer

Notes:

TEMPERATURE

MINUTES

Protein:	Cals:	Carbs:	Fat:

Check Box ✓	Vegitarian:	Vegan:	Gluten free:	Contains Nuts:	Lactose
	☐	☐	☐	☐	☐

Recipe .... ♥♥

Date ....

Serves .... Preperation time .... Cooking time ....

Ingredients

Directions

Air Fryer

TEMPERATURE

MINUTES

Notes:

Protein:	Cals:	Carbs:	Fat:

Check Box ✓	Vegitarian:	Vegan:	Gluten free:	Contains Nuts:	Lactose
	☐	☐	☐	☐	☐

Recipe -----------------------------

Date ....

Serves .... Preperation time .... Cooking time ....

Ingredients

Directions

Air Fryer

TEMPERATURE

MINUTES

Notes:

Protein:	Cals:	Carbs:	Fat:

Check Box ✓	Vegitarian:	Vegan:	Gluten free:	Contains Nuts:	Lactose
	☐	☐	☐	☐	☐

Recipe .... ♥♥

Date ....

Serves .... Preperation time .... Cooking time ....

Ingredients

Directions

_____

_____

_____

_____

_____

_____

_____

_____

_____

_____

_____

_____

_____

Notes:

Air Fryer

TEMPERATURE

MINUTES

Protein: **Cals:** **Carbs:** **Fat:**

Check Box ✓ | Vegitarian: | Vegan: | Gluten free: | Contains Nuts: | Lactose

☐ ☐ ☐ ☐ ☐

Recipe ------------------------------

Date ....

Serves .... Preperation time .... Cooking time ....

Ingredients

Directions

_____
_____
_____
_____
_____
_____
_____
_____
_____
_____
_____

Air Fryer

_____

TEMPERATURE

MINUTES

Notes:

Protein:	Cals:	Carbs:	Fat:

	Vegitarian:	Vegan:	Gluten free:	Contains Nuts:	Lactose
Check Box ✓	☐	☐	☐	☐	☐

Recipe ....

Date ....

Serves .... Preperation time .... Cooking time ....

Ingredients

Directions

Notes:

Air Fryer

TEMPERATURE

MINUTES

Protein:	Cals:	Carbs:	Fat:

Check Box ✓

Vegitarian:	Vegan:	Gluten free:	Contains Nuts:	Lactose
☐	☐	☐	☐	☐

Recipe ------------------------------

Date ....

Serves .... Preperation time .... Cooking time ....

Ingredients

Directions

Air Fryer

TEMPERATURE

MINUTES

Notes:

Protein: **Cals:**   **Carbs:**   **Fat:**

Check Box ✓

Vegitarian:	Vegan:	Gluten free:	Contains Nuts:	Lactose
☐	☐	☐	☐	☐

Recipe ....

Date ....

Serves .... Preperation time .... Cooking time ....

Ingredients

Directions

Air Fryer

TEMPERATURE

MINUTES

Notes:

Protein: **Cals:**   **Carbs:**   **Fat:**

Check Box ✓

Vegitarian:	Vegan:	Gluten free:	Contains Nuts:	Lactose
☐	☐	☐	☐	☐

Recipe --------------------------------

Date ....

Serves .... Preperation time .... Cooking time ....

Ingredients   ## Directions

Air Fryer

Notes:

TEMPERATURE

MINUTES

Protein:	Cals:	Carbs:	Fat:

Check Box ✓	Vegitarian:	Vegan:	Gluten free:	Contains Nuts:	Lactose
	☐	☐	☐	☐	☐

Recipe ------------------------------

Date ....

Serves .... Preperation time .... Cooking time ....

Ingredients   ## Directions

_____

Air Fryer

TEMPERATURE
MINUTES

Notes:

Protein: **Cals:**   **Carbs:**   **Fat:**

Check Box ✓

Vegitarian:	Vegan:	Gluten free:	Contains Nuts:	Lactose
☐	☐	☐	☐	☐

Recipe ------------------------------

Date ....

Serves .... Preperation time .... Cooking time ....

Ingredients

Directions

Notes;

Air Fryer

TEMPERATURE

MINUTES

Protein:	Cals:	Carbs:	Fat:

Check Box ✓

Vegitarian:	Vegan:	Gluten free:	Contains Nuts:	Lactose
☐	☐	☐	☐	☐

Recipe ....

Date ....

Serves .... Preperation time .... Cooking time ....

Ingredients

Directions

Air Fryer

Notes:

TEMPERATURE

MINUTES

Protein:	Cals:	Carbs:	Fat:

Check Box ✓	Vegitarian:	Vegan:	Gluten free:	Contains Nuts:	Lactose
	☐	☐	☐	☐	☐

Recipe

Date

Serves .... Preperation time .... Cooking time ....

Ingredients

Directions

Air Fryer

TEMPERATURE

MINUTES

Notes:

Protein:	Cals:	Carbs:	Fat:

Check Box ✓	Vegitarian:	Vegan:	Gluten free:	Contains Nuts:	Lactose
	☐	☐	☐	☐	☐

Recipe ······································

Date ····························

Serves ··········· Preperation time ················· Cooking time ·················

Ingredients

Directions

_____

_____

_____

_____

_____

_____

_____

_____

_____

_____

_____

_____

_____

Notes:

Air Fryer

TEMPERATURE

MINUTES

Protein;   **Cals;**   **Carbs;**   **Fat;**

Check Box ✓

Vegitarian:	Vegan;	Gluten free;	Contains Nuts;	Lactose
☐	☐	☐	☐	☐

Recipe ------------------------------

Date ....

Serves .... Preperation time .... Cooking time ....

Ingredients

Directions

Notes:

Air Fryer

TEMPERATURE

MINUTES

Protein:	Cals:	Carbs:	Fat:

Check Box ✓	Vegitarian:	Vegan:	Gluten free:	Contains Nuts:	Lactose
	☐	☐	☐	☐	☐

Recipe ....

Date ....

Serves .... Preperation time .... Cooking time ....

Ingredients

Directions

_____
_____
_____
_____
_____
_____
_____
_____
_____
_____
_____

Air Fryer

Notes:

TEMPERATURE

MINUTES

Protein: **Cals:**   **Carbs:**   **Fat:**

Check Box ✓   Vegitarian: Vegan: Gluten free: Contains Nuts: Lactose

☐   ☐   ☐   ☐   ☐

Recipe ----------------------------

Date ....

Serves .... Preperation time .... Cooking time ....

Ingredients

Directions

Notes:

Air Fryer

TEMPERATURE

MINUTES

Protein: **Cals:**   **Carbs:**   **Fat:**

Check Box ✓   Vegitarian: ☐   Vegan: ☐   Gluten free: ☐   Contains Nuts: ☐   Lactose ☐

Recipe ------------------------------

Date ....

Serves .... Preperation time .... Cooking time ....

Ingredients

Directions

Air Fryer

Notes:

TEMPERATURE

MINUTES

Protein: **Cals:**   **Carbs:**   **Fat:**

Check Box ✓   Vegitarian: Vegan: Gluten free: Contains Nuts: Lactose

| | | | | |

Recipe -------------------------------

Date ....

Serves .... Preperation time .... Cooking time ....

Ingredients   ## Directions

_____   _____
_____   _____
_____   _____
_____   _____
_____   _____
_____   _____
_____   _____
_____   _____
_____   _____
_____   _____
_____   _____
_____   Notes:
Air Fryer   _____
_____   _____
TEMPERATURE   _____
MINUTES

Protein: _____ **Cals:** _____ **Carbs:** _____ **Fat:** _____

Check Box ✓

Vegitarian:	Vegan:	Gluten free:	Contains Nuts:	Lactose
☐	☐	☐	☐	☐

Recipe ------------------------------

Date ....

Serves .... Preperation time .... Cooking time ....

Ingredients   ## Directions

_____
_____
_____
_____
_____
_____
_____
_____
_____
_____
_____
_____
_____

Notes:

Air Fryer

TEMPERATURE
MINUTES

Protein;	Cals;	Carbs;	Fat;

Check Box ✓	Vegitarian:	Vegan:	Gluten free:	Contains Nuts:	Lactose
	☐	☐	☐	☐	☐

Recipe ---------------------------------

Date ....

Serves .... Preperation time .... Cooking time ....

Ingredients

Directions

Notes:

Air Fryer

TEMPERATURE

MINUTES

Protein: Cals: Carbs: Fat:

Check Box ✓

Vegitarian:	Vegan:	Gluten free:	Contains Nuts:	Lactose
☐	☐	☐	☐	☐

Recipe ------------------------------

Date ....

Serves .... Preperation time .... Cooking time ....

Ingredients

Directions

Air Fryer

Notes:

TEMPERATURE

MINUTES

Protein:	Cals:	Carbs:	Fat:

Check Box ✓	Vegitarian:	Vegan:	Gluten free:	Contains Nuts:	Lactose
	☐	☐	☐	☐	☐

Recipe ------------------------------

Date ....

Serves .... Preperation time .... Cooking time ....

Ingredients

Directions

Notes:

Air Fryer

TEMPERATURE

MINUTES

Protein:	Cals:	Carbs:	Fat:

Check Box ✓

Vegitarian:	Vegan:	Gluten free:	Contains Nuts:	Lactose
☐	☐	☐	☐	☐

Recipe ------------------------------

Date ....

Serves .... Preperation time .... Cooking time ....

Ingredients

Directions

Air Fryer

TEMPERATURE

MINUTES

Notes:

Protein:	Cals:	Carbs:	Fat:

Check Box ✓	Vegitarian:	Vegan:	Gluten free:	Contains Nuts:	Lactose
	☐	☐	☐	☐	☐

Recipe ------------------------------

Date ....

Serves .... Preperation time .... Cooking time ....

Ingredients

Directions

Air Fryer

TEMPERATURE

MINUTES

Notes:

Protein: **Cals:**   **Carbs:**   **Fat:**

Check Box ✓

Vegitarian:	Vegan:	Gluten free:	Contains Nuts:	Lactose
☐	☐	☐	☐	☐

Recipe _____

Date ....

Serves .... Preperation time .... Cooking time ....

Ingredients   ## Directions

_____

Air Fryer

Notes:

TEMPERATURE

MINUTES

Protein:	Cals:	Carbs:	Fat:

Check Box ✓	Vegitarian:	Vegan:	Gluten free:	Contains Nuts:	Lactose
	☐	☐	☐	☐	☐

Recipe ----------------------------- ♥♥

Date ....

Serves .... Preperation time .... Cooking time ....

Ingredients

Directions

Air Fryer

Notes:

TEMPERATURE

MINUTES

Protein:	Cals:	Carbs:	Fat:

Check Box ✓

Vegitarian:	Vegan:	Gluten free:	Contains Nuts:	Lactose
☐	☐	☐	☐	☐

Recipe .... 🖤🖤

Date ....

Serves .... Preperation time .... Cooking time ....

Ingredients   ## Directions

_____   _____
_____   _____
_____   _____
_____   _____
_____   _____
_____   _____
_____   _____
_____   _____
_____   _____
_____   _____
_____   _____
_____   Notes:
_____   _____
Air Fryer   _____
TEMPERATURE   _____
MINUTES

Protein:	Cals:	Carbs:	Fat:

Check Box ✓	Vegitarian:	Vegan:	Gluten free:	Contains Nuts:	Lactose
	☐	☐	☐	☐	☐

Recipe ------------------------------

Date ....

Serves .... Preperation time .... Cooking time ....

Ingredients

Directions

Notes:

Air Fryer

TEMPERATURE

MINUTES

Protein:	Cals:	Carbs:	Fat:

Check Box ✓	Vegitarian:	Vegan:	Gluten free:	Contains Nuts:	Lactose
	☐	☐	☐	☐	☐

Recipe ....

Date ....

Serves .... Preperation time .... Cooking time ....

Ingredients   ## Directions

Air Fryer

Notes:

TEMPERATURE

MINUTES

Protein:	Cals:	Carbs:	Fat:

Check Box ✓	Vegitarian:	Vegan:	Gluten free:	Contains Nuts:	Lactose
	☐	☐	☐	☐	☐

Recipe ------------------------------

Date ....

Serves .... Preperation time .... Cooking time ....

Ingredients   ## Directions

_____   _____
_____   _____
_____   _____
_____   _____
_____   _____
_____   _____
_____   _____
_____   _____
_____   _____
_____   _____
_____   Notes:
Air Fryer   _____
_____   _____
TEMPERATURE
MINUTES

Protein: **Cals:**   **Carbs:**   **Fat:**

Check Box ✓   Vegitarian: □   Vegan: □   Gluten free: □   Contains Nuts: □   Lactose □

Recipe .... 🖤🖤

Date ....

Serves .... Preperation time .... Cooking time ....

Ingredients

Directions

Air Fryer

TEMPERATURE

MINUTES

Notes:

Protein:	Cals:	Carbs:	Fat:

Check Box ✓	Vegitarian:	Vegan:	Gluten free:	Contains Nuts:	Lactose
	☐	☐	☐	☐	☐

Recipe

....

Date ....

Serves .... Preperation time .... Cooking time ....

Ingredients

Directions

Air Fryer

Notes:

TEMPERATURE

MINUTES

Protein:	Cals:	Carbs:	Fat:

Check Box ✓

Vegitarian:	Vegan:	Gluten free:	Contains Nuts:	Lactose
☐	☐	☐	☐	☐

Recipe ....

Date ....

Serves .... Preperation time .... Cooking time ....

Ingredients

Directions

Air Fryer

TEMPERATURE

MINUTES

Notes:

Protein: Cals: Carbs: Fat:

Check Box ✓   Vegitarian: Vegan: Gluten free: Contains Nuts: Lactose

Recipe ------------------------------

Date ....

Serves .... Preperation time .... Cooking time ....

Ingredients

Directions

Notes:

Air Fryer

TEMPERATURE

MINUTES

Protein:	Cals:	Carbs:	Fat:

Check Box ✓	Vegitarian:	Vegan:	Gluten free:	Contains Nuts:	Lactose
	☐	☐	☐	☐	☐

Recipe ....

Date ....

Serves .... Preperation time .... Cooking time ....

Ingredients

Directions

Air Fryer

Notes:

TEMPERATURE

MINUTES

Protein: **Cals:**   **Carbs:**   **Fat:**

Check Box ✓

Vegitarian:	Vegan:	Gluten free:	Contains Nuts:	Lactose
☐	☐	☐	☐	☐

Recipe ------------------------------

Date ....

Serves .... Preperation time .... Cooking time ....

Ingredients

Directions

Notes:

Air Fryer

TEMPERATURE

MINUTES

Protein:	Cals:	Carbs:	Fat:

Check Box ✓	Vegitarian:	Vegan:	Gluten free:	Contains Nuts:	Lactose
	☐	☐	☐	☐	☐

Recipe ....

Date ....

Serves .... Preperation time .... Cooking time ....

Ingredients

Directions

Air Fryer

Notes:

TEMPERATURE

MINUTES

Protein: Cals: Carbs: Fat:

Check Box ✓

Vegitarian:	Vegan:	Gluten free:	Contains Nuts:	Lactose
☐	☐	☐	☐	☐

Recipe --------------------------------

Date ....

Serves .... Preperation time .... Cooking time ....

Ingredients

Directions

Notes:

Air Fryer

TEMPERATURE

MINUTES

Protein:	Cals:	Carbs:	Fat:

Check Box ✓	Vegitarian:	Vegan:	Gluten free:	Contains Nuts:	Lactose
	☐	☐	☐	☐	☐

Recipe

Date ....

Serves .... Preperation time .... Cooking time ....

Ingredients

Directions

Air Fryer

TEMPERATURE

MINUTES

Notes:

Protein:	Cals:	Carbs:	Fat:

Check Box ✓	Vegitarian:	Vegan:	Gluten free:	Contains Nuts:	Lactose
	☐	☐	☐	☐	☐

Recipe ------------------------------

Date ....

Serves .... Preperation time .... Cooking time ....

Ingredients   ## Directions

Air Fryer

Notes:

TEMPERATURE

MINUTES

Protein: **Cals:**   **Carbs:**   **Fat:**

Check Box ✓

Vegitarian:	Vegan:	Gluten free:	Contains Nuts:	Lactose
☐	☐	☐	☐	☐

Recipe ....

Date ....

Serves .... Preperation time .... Cooking time ....

Ingredients

Directions

Air Fryer

Notes:

TEMPERATURE

MINUTES

Protein:	Cals:	Carbs:	Fat:

Check Box ✓	Vegitarian:	Vegan:	Gluten free:	Contains Nuts:	Lactose
	☐	☐	☐	☐	☐

Recipe ----------------------------- ♥♥

Date ....

Serves .... **Preperation time** .... **Cooking time** ....

Ingredients

Directions

Notes:

Air Fryer

TEMPERATURE

MINUTES

Protein:	Cals:	Carbs:	Fat:

Check Box ✓	Vegitarian:	Vegan:	Gluten free:	Contains Nuts:	Lactose
	☐	☐	☐	☐	☐

Recipe ....

Date ....

Serves .... Preperation time .... Cooking time ....

Ingredients

Directions

Notes:

Air Fryer

TEMPERATURE

MINUTES

Protein: **Cals:**   **Carbs:**   **Fat:**

Check Box ✓

Vegitarian:	Vegan:	Gluten free:	Contains Nuts:	Lactose
☐	☐	☐	☐	☐

Recipe ------------------------------

Date ....

Serves .... Preperation time .... Cooking time ....

Ingredients

Directions

Air Fryer

TEMPERATURE

MINUTES

Notes:

Protein: Cals: Carbs: Fat:

Check Box ✓	Vegitarian:	Vegan:	Gluten free:	Contains Nuts:	Lactose
	☐	☐	☐	☐	☐

Recipe ----------------------------

Date ....

Serves .... Preperation time .... Cooking time ....

Ingredients

Directions

Notes:

Air Fryer

TEMPERATURE

MINUTES

Protein:	Cals:	Carbs:	Fat:

Check Box ✓	Vegitarian:	Vegan:	Gluten free:	Contains Nuts:	Lactose
	☐	☐	☐	☐	☐

Recipe ------------------------------

Date ....

Serves .... Preperation time .... Cooking time ....

Ingredients

Directions

Notes:

Air Fryer

TEMPERATURE

MINUTES

Protein:	Cals:	Carbs:	Fat:

Check Box ✓	Vegitarian:	Vegan:	Gluten free:	Contains Nuts:	Lactose
	☐	☐	☐	☐	☐

Recipe ....

Date ....

Serves .... Preperation time .... Cooking time ....

Ingredients

Directions

Notes:

Air Fryer

TEMPERATURE

MINUTES

Protein:	Cals:	Carbs:	Fat:	
Check Box ✓	Vegitarian:	Vegan:	Gluten free:	Contains Nuts:	Lactose

Recipe ------------------------------

Date ....

Serves .... Preperation time .... Cooking time ....

Ingredients

Directions

_____

_____

_____

_____

_____

_____

_____

_____

_____

_____

_____

_____

Notes:

Air Fryer

TEMPERATURE

MINUTES

Protein: **Cals:** **Carbs:** **Fat:**

Check Box ✓ | Vegitarian: | Vegan: | Gluten free: | Contains Nuts: | Lactose

Recipe ....

Date ....

Serves .... Preperation time .... Cooking time ....

Ingredients

Directions

Notes:

Air Fryer

TEMPERATURE

MINUTES

Protein: **Cals:**   **Carbs:**   **Fat:**

Check Box ✓ | Vegitarian: | Vegan: | Gluten free: | Contains Nuts: | Lactose

Recipe ----------------------------------

Date ....

Serves .... Preperation time .... Cooking time ....

Ingredients   ## Directions

_____   _____
_____   _____
_____   _____
_____   _____
_____   _____
_____   _____
_____   _____
_____   _____
_____   _____
_____   _____
_____   _____
_____   Notes:
Air Fryer   _____
                                 _____
TEMPERATURE   _____
MINUTES

Protein:	Cals:	Carbs:	Fat:

Check Box ✓ Vegitarian: Vegan: Gluten free: Contains Nuts: Lactose
☐   ☐   ☐   ☐   ☐

Recipe .... 🖤

Date ....

Serves .... Preperation time .... Cooking time ....

Ingredients   ## Directions

_____   _____
_____   _____
_____   _____
_____   _____
_____   _____
_____   _____
_____   _____
_____   _____
_____   _____
_____   _____
_____   _____
_____   Notes:
_____   _____
Air Fryer   _____
_____   _____
TEMPERATURE   _____
MINUTES

Protein:	Cals:	Carbs:	Fat:

Check Box ✓

Vegitarian:	Vegan:	Gluten free:	Contains Nuts:	Lactose
☐	☐	☐	☐	☐

Recipe _____

Date ....

Serves .... Preperation time .... Cooking time ....

Ingredients

Directions

_____
_____
_____
_____
_____
_____
_____
_____
_____
_____
_____
_____

Air Fryer

TEMPERATURE

MINUTES

Notes:

Protein:	Cals:	Carbs:	Fat:

Check Box ✓

Vegitarian:	Vegan:	Gluten free:	Contains Nuts:	Lactose
☐	☐	☐	☐	☐

Recipe ....

Date ....

Serves .... Preperation time .... Cooking time ....

Ingredients

Directions

_____

_____

_____

_____

_____

_____

_____

_____

_____

_____

_____

_____

Notes:

Air Fryer

TEMPERATURE

MINUTES

Protein: **Cals:**   **Carbs:**   **Fat:**

Check Box ✓

Vegitarian:	Vegan:	Gluten free:	Contains Nuts:	Lactose
☐	☐	☐	☐	☐

Recipe ------------------------------

Date ....

Serves .... Preperation time .... Cooking time ....

Ingredients   ## Directions

Air Fryer

TEMPERATURE

MINUTES

Notes:

Protein:	Cals:	Carbs:	Fat:

Check Box ✓

Vegitarian:	Vegan:	Gluten free:	Contains Nuts:	Lactose

Recipe ----------------------------- ♥♥

Date ....

Serves .... Preperation time .... Cooking time ....

Ingredients   ## Directions

_____
_____
_____
_____
_____
_____
_____
_____
_____
_____
_____
_____

Notes:

Air Fryer

TEMPERATURE
MINUTES

Protein:	Cals:	Carbs:	Fat:

Check Box ✓	Vegitarian:	Vegan:	Gluten free:	Contains Nuts:	Lactose
	☐	☐	☐	☐	☐

Recipe ------------------------------

Date ....

Serves .... Preperation time .... Cooking time ....

Ingredients

Directions

Notes:

Air Fryer

TEMPERATURE

MINUTES

Protein:	Cals:	Carbs:	Fat:

Check Box ✓

Vegitarian:	Vegan:	Gluten free:	Contains Nuts:	Lactose
☐	☐	☐	☐	☐

Recipe ------------------------------

Date ....

Serves .... Preperation time .... Cooking time ....

Ingredients

Directions

_____

_____

_____

_____

_____

_____

_____

_____

_____

_____

_____

Notes:

Air Fryer

TEMPERATURE

MINUTES

Protein:	Cals:	Carbs:	Fat:

Check Box ✓

Vegitarian:	Vegan:	Gluten free:	Contains Nuts:	Lactose
☐	☐	☐	☐	☐

Recipe -----------------------------

Date ....

Serves .... Preperation time .... Cooking time ....

Ingredients   ## Directions

_____   _____
_____   _____
_____   _____
_____   _____
_____   _____
_____   _____
_____   _____
_____   _____
_____   _____
_____   _____
_____   _____
_____   _____
_____   _____
_____   Notes:
_____   _____
Air Fryer   _____
_____   _____
TEMPERATURE   _____
MINUTES

Protein:	Cals:	Carbs:	Fat:

Check Box ✓ Vegitarian: Vegan: Gluten free: Contains Nuts: Lactose

☐ ☐ ☐ ☐ ☐

Recipe ....

Date ....

Serves .... Preperation time .... Cooking time ....

Ingredients

Directions

_____
_____
_____
_____
_____
_____
_____
_____
_____
_____
_____
_____
_____
_____

Air Fryer

TEMPERATURE

MINUTES

Notes:

Protein:	Cals:	Carbs:	Fat:	
Check Box ✓	Vegitarian:	Vegan:	Gluten free:	Contains Nuts:	Lactose
	☐	☐	☐	☐	☐

Recipe ------------------------------

Date ....

Serves .... Preperation time .... Cooking time ....

Ingredients

Directions

Air Fryer

TEMPERATURE

MINUTES

Notes:

Protein: Cals: Carbs: Fat:

Check Box ✓

Vegitarian:	Vegan:	Gluten free:	Contains Nuts:	Lactose
☐	☐	☐	☐	☐

Recipe .... ♥♥

Date ....

Serves .... Preperation time .... Cooking time ....

Ingredients   ## Directions

_____
_____
_____
_____
_____
_____
_____
_____
_____
_____
_____
_____

Notes:

Air Fryer

TEMPERATURE
MINUTES

Protein: **Cals:**   **Carbs:**   **Fat:**

Check Box ✓   Vegitarian: Vegan: Gluten free: Contains Nuts: Lactose

Recipe ------------------------------

Date ....

Serves .... Preperation time .... Cooking time ....

Ingredients

Directions

Notes:

Air Fryer

TEMPERATURE

MINUTES

Protein:	Cals:	Carbs:	Fat:

Check Box ✓	Vegitarian;	Vegan;	Gluten free;	Contains Nuts;	Lactose
	☐	☐	☐	☐	☐

Recipe ----------------------------------

Date ....

Serves .... Preperation time .... Cooking time ....

Ingredients   ## Directions

_____
_____
_____
_____
_____
_____
_____
_____
_____
_____
_____
_____

Notes:

Air Fryer

TEMPERATURE

MINUTES

Protein: **Cals:**   **Carbs:**   **Fat:**

Check Box ✓

Vegitarian:	Vegan:	Gluten free:	Contains Nuts:	Lactose
☐	☐	☐	☐	☐

Recipe ----------------------------- 🖤🖤

Date ....

Serves .... Preperation time .... Cooking time ....

Ingredients   ## Directions

_____   _____
_____   _____
_____   _____
_____   _____
_____   _____
_____   _____
_____   _____
_____   _____
_____   _____
_____   _____
_____   _____
_____   _____
_____   Notes:
_____   _____
Air Fryer   _____
_____   _____
TEMPERATURE   _____
MINUTES

Protein:	Cals:	Carbs:	Fat:

Check Box ✓

Vegitarian:	Vegan:	Gluten free:	Contains Nuts:	Lactose
☐	☐	☐	☐	☐

Recipe _____

Date ....

Serves .... Preperation time .... Cooking time ....

Ingredients

Directions

Air Fryer

TEMPERATURE

MINUTES

Notes:

Protein: **Cals:**   **Carbs:**   **Fat:**

Check Box ✓

Vegitarian:	Vegan:	Gluten free:	Contains Nuts:	Lactose
☐	☐	☐	☐	☐

Recipe -----------------------------

Date ....

Serves .... Preperation time .... Cooking time ....

Ingredients   ## Directions

Notes:

Air Fryer

TEMPERATURE

MINUTES

Protein:	Cals:	Carbs:	Fat:

Check Box ✓ | Vegitarian: | Vegan: | Gluten free: | Contains Nuts: | Lactose

Recipe ----------------------------------- ♥♥

Date ....

Serves .... Preperation time .... Cooking time ....

Ingredients

Directions

Air Fryer

TEMPERATURE

MINUTES

Notes;

Protein;   **Cals;**   **Carbs;**   **Fat;**

Check Box ✓ | Vegitarian; | Vegan; | Gluten free; | Contains Nuts; | Lactose

Recipe ------------------------------

Date ....

Serves .... Preperation time .... Cooking time ....

Ingredients   ## Directions

Air Fryer

Notes:

TEMPERATURE

MINUTES

Protein:	Cals:	Carbs:		Fat:
Check Box ✓	Vegitarian:	Vegan:	Gluten free:	Contains Nuts:	Lactose
	☐	☐	☐	☐	☐

Recipe ---------------------------------

Date ....

Serves .... Preperation time .... Cooking time ....

Ingredients   ## Directions

Air Fryer

TEMPERATURE

MINUTES

Notes:

Protein:	Cals:	Carbs:	Fat:

Check Box ✔

Vegitarian:	Vegan:	Gluten free:	Contains Nuts:	Lactose
☐	☐	☐	☐	☐

Recipe ....

Date ....

Serves .... Preperation time .... Cooking time ....

Ingredients

Directions

Air Fryer

TEMPERATURE

MINUTES

Notes:

Protein: **Cals:**   **Carbs:**   **Fat:**

Check Box ✓

Vegitarian;	Vegan;	Gluten free;	Contains Nuts;	Lactose
☐	☐	☐	☐	☐

Recipe ....

Date ....

Serves .... Preperation time .... Cooking time ....

Ingredients   ## Directions

_____
_____
_____
_____
_____
_____
_____
_____
_____
_____
_____
_____

Notes:

Air Fryer

TEMPERATURE

MINUTES

Protein: **Cals:**   **Carbs:**   **Fat:**

Check Box ✓   Vegitarian: Vegan: Gluten free: Contains Nuts: Lactose

Recipe ------------------------------

Date ....

Serves .... Preperation time .... Cooking time ....

Ingredients

Directions

Notes:

Air Fryer

TEMPERATURE

MINUTES

Protein:	Cals:	Carbs:	Fat:

Check Box ✓	Vegitarian:	Vegan:	Gluten free:	Contains Nuts:	Lactose
	☐	☐	☐	☐	☐

Recipe ------------------------------

Date ....

Serves .... Preperation time .... Cooking time ....

Ingredients

Directions

_____
_____
_____
_____
_____
_____
_____
_____
_____
_____
_____
_____
_____

Notes:

Air Fryer

TEMPERATURE

MINUTES

Protein:	Cals:	Carbs:	Fat:

Check Box ✓	Vegitarian:	Vegan:	Gluten free:	Contains Nuts:	Lactose
	☐	☐	☐	☐	☐

Recipe ------------------------------

Date ....

Serves .... Preperation time .... Cooking time ....

Ingredients   ## Directions

Air Fryer

Notes:

TEMPERATURE

MINUTES

Protein: **Cals:**   **Carbs:**   **Fat:**

Check Box ✓   Vegitarian: ☐   Vegan: ☐   Gluten free: ☐   Contains Nuts: ☐   Lactose ☐

Recipe -----------------------------

Date ....

Serves .... Preperation time .... Cooking time ....

Ingredients

Directions

Air Fryer

TEMPERATURE

MINUTES

Notes:

Protein: **Cals:**   **Carbs:**   **Fat:**

Check Box ✓   Vegitarian: Vegan: Gluten free: Contains Nuts: Lactose

☐ ☐ ☐ ☐ ☐

Recipe -------------------------------

Date ....

Serves .... Preperation time .... Cooking time ....

Ingredients

Directions

Air Fryer

TEMPERATURE

MINUTES

Notes:

Protein: **Cals:**   **Carbs:**   **Fat:**

Check Box ✓

Vegitarian:	Vegan:	Gluten free:	Contains Nuts:	Lactose
☐	☐	☐	☐	☐

Recipe ------------------------------------

Date ....

Serves .... Preperation time .... Cooking time ....

Ingredients   ## Directions

Air Fryer

Notes:

TEMPERATURE

MINUTES

Protein: **Cals:**   **Carbs:**   **Fat:**

Check Box ✓   Vegitarian: Vegan: Gluten free: Contains Nuts: Lactose

☐   ☐   ☐   ☐   ☐

Recipe ------------------------------

Date ....

Serves .... Preperation time .... Cooking time ....

Ingredients

Directions

Notes:

Air Fryer

TEMPERATURE

MINUTES

Protein:	Cals:	Carbs:	Fat:

Check Box ✓	Vegitarian:	Vegan:	Gluten free:	Contains Nuts:	Lactose
	☐	☐	☐	☐	☐

Recipe _____

Date ....

Serves .... Preperation time .... Cooking time ....

Ingredients

Directions

Notes:

Air Fryer

TEMPERATURE

MINUTES

Protein:	Cals:	Carbs:	Fat:

Check Box ✓

Vegitarian:	Vegan:	Gluten free:	Contains Nuts:	Lactose
☐	☐	☐	☐	☐

Recipe ------------------------------

Date ....

Serves .... Preperation time .... Cooking time ....

Ingredients

Directions

Air Fryer

TEMPERATURE

MINUTES

Notes:

Protein:	Cals:	Carbs:	Fat:

Check Box ✓

Vegitarian:	Vegan:	Gluten free:	Contains Nuts:	Lactose
☐	☐	☐	☐	☐

Recipe ....

Date ....

Serves .... Preperation time .... Cooking time ....

Ingredients

Directions

Air Fryer

TEMPERATURE

MINUTES

Notes:

Protein: **Cals:**   **Carbs:**   **Fat:**

Check Box ✓

Vegitarian:	Vegan:	Gluten free:	Contains Nuts:	Lactose
☐	☐	☐	☐	☐

Recipe _____

Date ....

Serves .... Preperation time .... Cooking time ....

Ingredients

Directions

Air Fryer

TEMPERATURE

MINUTES

Notes:

Protein:	Cals:	Carbs:	Fat:

Check Box ✓	Vegitarian:	Vegan:	Gluten free:	Contains Nuts:	Lactose
	☐	☐	☐	☐	☐

Recipe ----------------------------------

Date ....

Serves .... Preperation time .... Cooking time ....

Ingredients

Directions

Air Fryer

TEMPERATURE

MINUTES

Notes:

Protein: **Cals:**   **Carbs:**   **Fat:**

Check Box ✓

Vegitarian:	Vegan:	Gluten free:	Contains Nuts:	Lactose
☐	☐	☐	☐	☐

Recipe ------------------------------

Date ....

Serves .... Preperation time .... Cooking time ....

Ingredients

Directions

Air Fryer

TEMPERATURE

MINUTES

Notes:

Protein:	Cals:	Carbs:	Fat:

Check Box ✓

Vegitarian:	Vegan:	Gluten free:	Contains Nuts:	Lactose
☐	☐	☐	☐	☐

Recipe ·································

Date ························

Serves ··········· Preperation time ················ Cooking time ················

Ingredients   ## Directions

Notes:

Air Fryer

TEMPERATURE
MINUTES

Protein:	Cals:	Carbs:	Fat:

Check Box ✓ | Vegitarian: | Vegan: | Gluten free: | Contains Nuts: | Lactose

Recipe ----------------------------- ♥♥

Date ....

Serves .... Preperation time .... Cooking time ....

Ingredients   ## Directions

_____   _____
_____   _____
_____   _____
_____   _____
_____   _____
_____   _____
_____   _____
_____   _____
_____   _____
_____   _____
_____   _____
_____   _____
_____   Notes:
Air Fryer   _____
_____   _____
TEMPERATURE   _____
MINUTES

Protein: **Cals:**   **Carbs:**   **Fat:**

Check Box ✓ | Vegitarian: ☐ | Vegan: ☐ | Gluten free: ☐ | Contains Nuts: ☐ | Lactose ☐

Recipe .... ❤❤

Date ....

Serves .... Preperation time .... Cooking time ....

Ingredients   ## Directions

Air Fryer

TEMPERATURE

MINUTES

Notes:

Protein:	Cals:	Carbs:	Fat:

Check Box ✓	Vegitarian:	Vegan:	Gluten free:	Contains Nuts:	Lactose
	☐	☐	☐	☐	☐

Recipe _____

Date ....

Serves .... Preperation time .... Cooking time ....

Ingredients

Directions

_____
_____
_____
_____
_____
_____
_____
_____
_____
_____
_____
_____
_____

Air Fryer

Notes:
_____

TEMPERATURE

MINUTES

Protein: **Cals:**   **Carbs:**   **Fat:**

Check Box ✓

Vegitarian;	Vegan;	Gluten free;	Contains Nuts;	Lactose
☐	☐	☐	☐	☐

Recipe ----------------------------------

Date ....

Serves .... Preperation time .... Cooking time ....

Ingredients

Directions

Air Fryer

Notes:

TEMPERATURE

MINUTES

Protein:	Cals:	Carbs:	Fat:

Check Box ✓	Vegitarian:	Vegan:	Gluten free:	Contains Nuts:	Lactose
	☐	☐	☐	☐	☐

Recipe ------------------------------

Date ....

Serves .... Preperation time .... Cooking time ....

Ingredients

Directions

Air Fryer

TEMPERATURE

MINUTES

Notes:

Protein:_____ Cals:_____ Carbs:_____ Fat:_____

Check Box ✓

Vegitarian:	Vegan:	Gluten free:	Contains Nuts:	Lactose
☐	☐	☐	☐	☐

Recipe _____

Date ....

Serves .... Preperation time .... Cooking time ....

Ingredients   ## Directions

_____
_____
_____
_____
_____
_____
_____
_____
_____
_____
_____
_____
_____

Notes:

Air Fryer

TEMPERATURE

MINUTES

Protein: **Cals:**   **Carbs:**   **Fat:**

Check Box ✓   Vegitarian: Vegan: Gluten free: Contains Nuts: Lactose

☐   ☐   ☐   ☐   ☐

Recipe --------------------------------

Date ....

Serves .... Preperation time .... Cooking time ....

Ingredients

Directions

_____

_____

_____

_____

_____

_____

_____

_____

_____

_____

_____

_____

_____

_____

_____

Air Fryer

TEMPERATURE

MINUTES

Notes:

Protein:	Cals:	Carbs:	Fat:

Check Box ✓	Vegitarian:	Vegan:	Gluten free:	Contains Nuts:	Lactose
	☐	☐	☐	☐	☐

Recipe ------------------------------

Date ....

Serves .... Preperation time .... Cooking time ....

Ingredients

Directions

Air Fryer

Notes:

TEMPERATURE

MINUTES

Protein: Cals: Carbs: Fat:

Check Box ✓   Vegitarian: Vegan: Gluten free: Contains Nuts: Lactose

☐   ☐   ☐   ☐   ☐

Recipe ----------------------------- ♥

Date ....

Serves .... Preperation time .... Cooking time ....

Ingredients

Directions

Air Fryer

TEMPERATURE

MINUTES

Notes:

Protein: Cals: Carbs: Fat:

Check Box ✓ | Vegitarian: | Vegan: | Gluten free: | Contains Nuts: | Lactose

Recipe ....

Date ....

Serves .... Preperation time .... Cooking time ....

Ingredients   ## Directions

_____
_____
_____
_____
_____
_____
_____
_____
_____
_____
_____
_____

Air Fryer

TEMPERATURE

MINUTES

Notes:

Protein: **Cals:**   **Carbs:**   **Fat:**

Check Box ✓   Vegitarian: ☐   Vegan: ☐   Gluten free: ☐   Contains Nuts: ☐   Lactose ☐

Recipe ----------------------------

Date ....

Serves .... Preperation time .... Cooking time ....

Ingredients

Directions

Notes:

Air Fryer

TEMPERATURE

MINUTES

Protein:	Cals:	Carbs:	Fat:

Check Box ✓	Vegitarian:	Vegan:	Gluten free:	Contains Nuts:	Lactose
	☐	☐	☐	☐	☐

Recipe .... 🖤

Date ....

Serves .... Preperation time .... Cooking time ....

Ingredients

Directions

_____

Air Fryer

TEMPERATURE

MINUTES

Notes:

Protein:	Cals:	Carbs:		Fat:

Check Box ✓

Vegitarian:	Vegan:	Gluten free:	Contains Nuts:	Lactose
☐	☐	☐	☐	☐

Recipe ----------------------------

Date ....

Serves .... Preperation time .... Cooking time ....

Ingredients

Directions

Air Fryer

TEMPERATURE

MINUTES

Notes:

Protein: Cals: Carbs: Fat:

Check Box ✓   Vegitarian: Vegan: Gluten free: Contains Nuts: Lactose

☐   ☐   ☐   ☐   ☐

Recipe ------------------------------

Date ....

Serves .... Preperation time .... Cooking time ....

Ingredients   ## Directions

Air Fryer

TEMPERATURE

MINUTES

Notes:

| Protein: | Cals: | Carbs: | Fat: |

Check Box ✓

Vegitarian:	Vegan:	Gluten free:	Contains Nuts:	Lactose
☐	☐	☐	☐	☐

Made in the USA
Middletown, DE
06 December 2022

17277174R00066